The Prenuptial Guide:
Contracts for Lovers

**David Greig and
Ross Davidson, LAWYERS**

Self-Counsel Press
(a division of)
International Self-Counsel Press Ltd.
USA   Canada

Self-Counsel Press acknowledges the financial support of the Government of Canada through the Canada Book Fund for our publishing activities.

Printed in Canada.

First edition: 2013

Library and Archives Canada Cataloguing in Publication

We regret that Cataloging In Publication (CIP) data had not been supplied to us when this book went to press, a month after we applied to Library and Archives Canada for the data.

Self-Counsel Press
(a division of)
International Self-Counsel Press Ltd.

Bellingham, WA   North Vancouver, BC
USA   Canada

Contents

Notice to Readers

Introduction

This book is intended to help parties plan for the future. It is intended to assist like-minded couples (or those who are about to become a couple) prepare a simple and enforceable agreement that will govern their legal affairs during the relationship, and determine what will happen if they separate.

A fairly negotiated, simple, written agreement does not need to cost thousands of dollars and take months to conclude. Having said that, this book is intended to provide general advice, and a simple sample agreement, to help parties who have relatively ordinary issues and modest concerns. If substantial capital assets, children's issues, tax- and estate-planning topics, or complex corporate law matters are involved, this book can provide some helpful preliminary advice, but eventually, you may need expert legal advice and help with the agreement.

As we have explained in the book, *The Separation Guide*, having a consultation with a lawyer does not need to be costly or oppressive. Most lawyers love to talk, and many offer free initial consultations. Your local Bar Association, Law School, or Law Society can provide help in finding a lawyer who will consult with you in regards to the topic of concern. The value of this resource should not be overlooked.

Conduct your own research and Internet investigations with caution: Bad information can go a long way.

This book can help lovers and spouses during their relationship, and to avoid the trauma, expense, and misery that often arises at the end of a relationship. It is not intended to discourage long-term romantic monogamy or hasten the end of healthy relationships. Nor should the topic dampen the passion of genuine romance. Instead, the purpose of this book — and the purpose of any prenuptial agreement or marriage contract — is to offer the participants peace of mind. A contract made by lovers, about their relationship, and what will happen if it ends, allows the parties to determine their fate in the event of separation *on their own terms*. An agreement about how a couple will live their lives together, and what will happen if they separate, can bring certainty, predictability, and comfort to a relationship. In a complex world where assets, liabilities, parental obligations, and legal conflict can threaten sanity, a simple agreement can offer calm.

This book is intended to serve as a guide for parties entering into new relationships. If, however, you are already involved in a lasting relationship, and want to take time to define the terms of your cohabitation, we can help — a "marriage contract" may be just what you need.

Our publication offers advice about how these agreements can be formed, and prepared, and provides a sample (general) agreement. It can help parties define the terms on which the relationship is to be based. Working through the materials in this book (together with your partner or on your own) will focus you on the issues, and illuminate topics of concern. Calm discussion about these matters *before* trouble erupts is wise. Sometimes it's best to plan for a rainy day whilst a sunny forecast prevails.

No one plans a picnic with showers in mind. Notwithstanding, every year, thousands of parties, cook-ups, and family reunions are ruined by an unexpected turn in the weather. More BBQs are destroyed by rain than by ants. Knowing this, thoughtful party planners anticipate the unexpected. They think about shelter solutions, alternate venues, indoor children's activities, and other options. They hope it doesn't rain at the event, but if it does, they have a backup plan. That backup plan does not mean it's more likely to rain on the day of the BBQ — it just means that there are alternatives if things go wrong.

Lovers tend not to plan for rain. The passionate immediacy of newfound love never dovetails with discussions about housing, vehicles, and children. The boyfriend who wants to talk about cohabitation agreements on a second date is likely on his final date. We (the authors) know this, because most of our income is earned acting for clients who failed to plan for possible rain in their relationship.

Talking about legal matters at the start of a romance may not be sexy, but it is smart. The complex legal arrangements that flow from a durable relationship can take parties by surprise, and create obligations that were unimaginable in the dating phase. In the modern Western world, planning ahead is not only responsible and prudent, it's necessary. If you are reading this at home, having purchased the book, you probably don't need much reassurance — you already appreciate that an agreement is a good idea. Accordingly, we won't waste any more paper trying to convince you of that any further — you must intuitively know that, or you wouldn't be reading this paragraph!

Unfortunately, this book can't help you broach the subject with your lover. The authors are lawyers, not counselors, and we have no special skill or ability in psychology. We can't offer tips about the best ways to weave law into a candlelit dinner. We have no "opening line" strategies, or top tips for dating conversation. We would suggest, however, that in a truly healthy relationship (even in the early stages), a calm and respectful discussion about legal matters should be possible. Raising the topic early on might even help convince your partner that you are serious about the relationship, and committed to being fair. Frankly, if you can't discuss the matter at all, you might want to return to "Plenty of Fish"!

1

Understanding the Difference between the Contracts

In this book, we use the terms prenuptial, marriage contract, and cohabitation agreement interchangeably to improve readability, but the fact of the matter is that the terminology is more a matter of perception, than substance. This book is intended to provide guidance about the topic (and a sample agreement) for parties who are in love and plan to live together. If you are entering into a contract to govern that kind of a relationship, it really matters little what the document is called. It can be simply entitled *agreement* or *contract* (and, in fact, that's what we recommend) and the effect will be the same.

However, you don't need this book, or an agreement similar to the precedent provided, if you are planning to reside with a friend as a roommate. This book is similarly inapplicable for neighbors who want to share boat ownership, and friends who are planning to jointly acquire a revenue property. Those parties may need a joint-venture agreement, a co-owners contract, a partnership agreement, or a corporation agreement, but they do not need a prenuptial contract, cohabitation agreement, or marriage contract.

Prenuptial contracts and marriage agreements share love as a common theme, and the intention to live together as lovers. That's what we're talking about in this publication — something that goes beyond the mere commerce of cooperation, and involves an emotional or psycho-social commitment. Romance is very often at the center of that. You may not be lovers at the end of the relationship (when you pull the agreement out for review as you part ways) but you should be lovers when you make the contract.

So, if you are only dating, do not live with your lover, and have no aspirations to do so, you can probably put this book down now.

1. What's the Difference between a Prenuptial Contract, Marriage Contract, and Cohabitation Agreement?

The following sections discuss the three different types of contracts.

1.1 Prenuptial contract

A prenuptial contract is an agreement that is entered into by parties (i.e., same sex or heterosexual) in anticipation of a planned date of marriage. It is intended to govern the affairs of the couple after their official matrimonial union, and will describe how they manage money, property, and children (if relevant), and how they will untangle these issues if they separate.

A prenuptial contract is often created where there is an imbalance between parties who are planning to marry, and one (or both) spouses want to protect their assets or their children, in the event that things don't work out. These are popular agreements with Hollywood stars, professional athletes, and those who wish they were one or the other.

1.2 Marriage contract

A marriage contract (sometimes called a "marriage agreement") is almost the same as a prenuptial contract, except that a marriage contract is typically made *during* or inside a marriage (rather than in anticipation of a marriage). In all other respects, a marriage agreement will achieve the same objectives mentioned in section **1.1**.

1.3 Cohabitation agreement

A cohabitation agreement is a contract between parties who intend to live together (or who are already living together), usually in a romantic and monogamous union, and who want to set out some principles about assets and liabilities and children and so on, in the absence of marriage. In those jurisdictions where same-sex couples cannot marry, a cohabitation agreement may be the only available contractual option.

In most jurisdictions, there still exists a significant legal distinction between the rights and obligations which apply to married people, and the rules for those who are cohabiting as spouses in a common-law relationship. Perceptions about this distinction are changing, as are the rules about marriage for same-sex couples. While this transition moves along (in some places at a glacial pace), it remains the case that married parties are often treated differently under the law than parties who are not married. So, for same-sex couples and for common-law spouses who have no intention to marry, a cohabitation agreement is the contract of choice.

2

Ground Rules

Your agreement is a contract so contract law principles apply. This chapter will supply you with some of the important ground rules for creating a contract.

1. When Should You Make the Agreement?

The best time to plan a picnic is in advance. Waiting to see what the weather will do on the day of the event is like checking the brakes on a car during a high-speed test drive. It's like that with contracts for lovers too.

While it is entirely possible to make an agreement after you have moved in together, committed to the relationship, and (even) after you have married, it may not be best to wait. We lawyers say that because we worry about legal problems that can lie in wait for the unwary. Besides, once you have set up housekeeping arrangements with your new spouse, some of the incentive for bargaining is gone, and some of the bargaining power has passed too.

When I take a holiday, I know where I'm going, when I'm going to return, and I generally have a rough idea of what I'll do along the way. I also buy travel insurance. While it may be possible to buy travel insurance part way through the journey, the choices (i.e., the insurance options) are far greater and more varied prior to departure.

If you move in with your lover, buy a vehicle together, obtain a joint line of credit, and then sit down to talk about a cohabitation agreement, there will quite possibly be fewer options and opportunities to negotiate freely. For instance, if it turns out, during the course of the discussion, that you really aren't like-minded on matters of commerce, the option of just "walking away" no longer exists. It is for that reason that we recommend that parties discuss the issues early in their relationship, and before their affairs become intertwined and complicated by joint and mutual obligations and responsibilities.

If that's not possible, and the first discussion about the topic occurs "after the lovin'," (or after the marriage, or after the second childbirth), it's not "too late," but it's not ideal. The perfect legal opportunity to settle the terms is before the complications arise, but we recognize that life isn't always perfect or simple. It is for that reason that parties quite often enter into marriage contracts part way through a relationship (and typically after marriage). Often, that's because their circumstances have changed. The parties start new careers, or are about to have a child, buy a house, move to a new country, receive an inheritance, or embark on some other new adventure. At such times, stipulating terms in a contract is wise.

Often, we lawyers are asked how long a couple can live together before they are "legally" connected. Usually, inquiries about this topic arise when a couple approach an important anniversary (at the end of their first or second year together) and one of them is beginning to wonder if the finances are now intertwined.

The rules about this vary from one jurisdiction to another. In some places, there is no entitlement to share in property until after the couple has cohabited for two years. In other places, it's a shorter or longer period of time — it just depends on residency. It is important to note, however, that the intertwining (or co-mingling) of legal obligations and responsibilities can start much earlier, in some circumstances, depending on the facts. For instance, if a young loving couple purchases a house together, and signs a mortgage together — for that purpose — it does not matter whether their relationship lasts for a year, five years, or an hour-and-a-half: They are bound and are jointly and severally liable by their ownership and their mortgage covenants. Likewise, a couple who parents a young child in the infancy of a relationship will have certain and specific obligations in regard to the child no matter how impermanent their love may be.

To summarize, the discussion about a contract should be conducted as soon as possible. Second, it's never too late to talk.

2. Some Basic Ground Rules

If you have determined that it does make sense to have a contract, there are some basic rules about construction of the document that should be observed. The following sections discuss these rules.

2.1 Get the contract in writing

To say, "get the contract in writing" sounds ridiculous, but an agreement (any contract) should be formally put down on paper. It may be obvious, but a great number of critical lawsuits, some involving millions of dollars, have been fought on the basis of *oral* agreements.

An interesting twist on this principle arose in my own practice once — a couple entered into a separation agreement, which was partly oral, and partly written in pencil. The magnitude of the silliness was compounded when the husband alleged that the wife had modified the agreement (by using an eraser) after they had divided accounts at the bank. The point is that anything worth remembering in contract law is worth having in writing … and use a *pen*!

2.2 Disclosure

One Canadian judge has described nondisclosure as the "cancer of matrimonial litigation." Nondisclosure of assets and liabilities is also, probably, the most common trouble spot in respect to cohabitation and other domestic contracts.

The principle of disclosure is a simple one, but often forgotten. It is this: If you are going to enter into a contract with your lover, and expect be bound by it, you are each entitled to know what you're getting into. Assets, liabilities, disabilities, obligations, income, and expenses should all be revealed. Candor and honesty are at the heart of these agreements, and the failure to fully and fairly disclose has been said to contaminate the very basis of the consent — and can (and usually will) invalidate the agreement. That does not mean that if you keep your vehicle loan a secret, you can "get out of" your marriage contract later. It does, however, probably mean that in the event that things don't work out, the vehicle loan will be yours alone. Other more harsh consequences may also follow.

The bottom line is that you must describe all matters of significance or legal import, and you must, at the very least, fully disclose matters that may be of interest to your spouse. Use the schedules at the back of the sample agreement to achieve this, and check them over at least three times before you sign anything.

2.3 Insure the agreement makes sense

Fancy legalese should have no part in your contract. Your contract is intended to be a fairly negotiated, plain and simple agreement between you and your spouse. If there is any language in the contract which is capable of misinterpretation, or is not plain and clear, remove it. Find a way to express your intentions in an understandable fashion, and avoid legalese.

Before you sign the agreement, read it three times, and then insure that your spouse has done the same. As a final test, have a friend read it, and then ask him or her to tell you what it means. If your understanding is not perfectly matched by the disinterested friend, it's time to go back to the drawing board.

2.4 Do you need a lawyer?

No, you don't "need" a lawyer, but in some cases, it might be smart to have a lawyer review your agreement before you sign it. It is always a good idea to retain a lawyer for document review if you are entering into a relationship with dependent children, have significant assets or liabilities, or if the prospect of enduring support and maintenance may be an issue. In such circumstances, you may not need to hire a lawyer to draft the agreement (you can likely still make use of the precedent in this book), but you may want a lawyer to examine your work and give you an opinion about it. This process (often referred to as the giving of "independent legal advice") can take 15 minutes to 1 hour, and might cost $50 to $350. It might be the best money you ever spend.

However, if you are young, have no dependents, and are starting your relationship without property or responsibility, it may not be necessary to retain counsel.

Note that the involvement of a lawyer does not guarantee enforceability, just as the absence of counsel's involvement does not forecast invalidity. A written contract, entered into by consenting adults with proper disclosure, is usually enforceable with or without a lawyer's involvement.

3
The Issues

When a spousal relationship comes to an end, there are typically five key issues to discuss:

- Custody of children
- Access to children
- Guardianship
- Maintenance or support
- Division of property

In many cases, there may be other questions too (e.g., possession of the home, division of bill payments, and ownership of jewelry, and valuables). Depending on the circumstances, one or more of these issues may be relevant on separation, and some may be of keen interest, contentious, or even problematic. Some may not matter at all.

We say this because these are the same concepts which need to be addressed at the outset of your relationship. Your contract needs to speak to the issues surrounding children, support, and property. You must explain how you will handle finances, and who will pay what.

You should address ownership of the house, and what support will be paid if you part ways. You are not required to describe every detail of daily life, and you are not expected or required to explain the minutiae of family finances. However, the "big picture" should be covered.

Some people want details, and try to explain their banking arrangements and describe every detail of their daily lives. This, typically, is impossible, unrewarding, and a bad idea. We discourage it. In general, the more specific the details, the more likely it is that there will be opportunity for mischief and misunderstanding.

With respect to monthly finances, for instance, a simple and workable approach might be to say something like this:

Les and Nat agree to maintain one joint bank account (together) for the management of their household expenses. They will each contribute similar amounts to that account to pay the household mortgage, phone, and Internet. At present, based on their circumstances, incomes, and expenses, it is agreed that Les and Nat will each pay $900 per month into that account, and from it, pay the mortgage, phone, and Internet. As their circumstances change, they will revisit and revise this arrangement, always having regard to the principle that they shall share these expenses fairly.

That's not beautiful prose, but it doesn't need to be. This is a contract that's about cooperation — not a submission for the Pulitzer. Your clauses must be plain, fair, and understandable, but they don't have to be beautiful. Work with the language until you have something that is clear and acceptable. Examine the sample agreement at the back of this book, and you'll see some options.

1. Custody, Access, and Guardianship of Children

With respect to the custody of and access to and guardianship of children, it is important to keep the following in mind:

- The law in almost all jurisdictions gives the court the discretion to vary an agreement or contract about children which is contrary to the best interest of the children. The language of the law on this topic is variable, but the principle is quite universal in North America. Keep this in mind as you consider the applicable clauses that will govern in your case.

- You probably do not need to describe, in your agreement, how you are going to parent the children while you are together and the relationship is thriving. Some folks want to do this, but it's never a great idea. I have seen, for instance, clauses that say "if we have any children, we agree to raise them as Christians" (or some such term), but these are rarely clever. You can't easily enforce a contract against a person who sleeps in your bed every night. However, your contract can describe what will happen to children in the event that the relationship ends, and as long as the clauses make sense and are generally in the best interests of the children, that's probably adequate.

• The language used to describe parenting arrangements (in a cohabitation contract) need not be legalese. In fact, we would all prefer the abolition of legalese altogether. Similarly, it is not necessary to employ words such as "custody," "residency," or "visitation." The central focus will be whether the description is understandable, fair, sensible, and in the best interests of the children. If you do not want to worry about sensitive language choices, simply say where the child will reside and when.

• It's not about the convenience or personal wishes of the parties — it's about what's best for the children. Agreements that say "Nat agrees never to see Les's children in the event of separation" are, predictably, largely unenforceable, unless there is something wrong with Nat or it's contrary to the welfare of the children for some demonstrable reason. Having said that, a fair agreement that gives one parent (usually the biological parent) some sort of primary residency or custodial edge may be quite enforceable, even in jurisdictions where joint-parenting presumptions reign. The facts and circumstances of each case will be paramount.

• Agreements which try to establish rules about existing children being brought into a new parental relationship (who are borne of a different parent) can be helpful. If the parties to the contract are able to agree on issues such as education, financial obligations, activity expenses, and other parenting issues, they may take some comfort in their arrangements. Many nuclear families might benefit from discussion about this, but somehow they find ways to deal with the issues without writing the terms down. Consider whether it is important to actually say anything at all. Not everything in life needs to be in writing.

- Any terms that are settled in the contract cannot purport to impose rules on nonparties. This will be of particular interest where the children described in the contact have a parenting arrangement with another parent or family. Be sure that your agreement does not inadvertently compromise the rights of some nonparty. Again, common sense should prevail.

2. Maintenance and Support

With respect to maintenance and support, there are several key principles.

First, keep in mind that there are many different types of spousal support. The most obvious and well known (monthly alimony or non-compensatory support) arises when one spouse has the means to pay support, and the other spouse has a need. Other types of support, including contractual support and compensatory maintenance, are based on different legal principles. Support of all kinds can be paid periodically or on a lump sum basis, but the usual arrangement is for monthly instalments.

Spousal support that is paid periodically (not in one lump sum) and which is paid pursuant to a written agreement or court order, is often tax deductible by the payor, and taxable income in the hands of the recipient. This distinction is important.

If your contract is intended to limit, oust, or preclude spousal support or maintenance of any type, and for all time, it must be plainly stated. Many prenuptial agreements have been made expressly for this purpose. For such a clause to stand up, you need clarity and specificity. A general paragraph will not withstand judicial scrutiny.

In addition, the proposition must be fair, and should be explained. A clause that might not survive review would be this:

Les, (aged 20) agrees the he will never seek spousal support from Nat.

Depending on how long Les and Nat are together, what happens to them, and how they fare in the world of capitalism, this clause may or may not be problematic.

A carefully crafted clause that is plain, fair, and supported by fact, is probably enforceable. For instance:

Les and Nat specifically acknowledge, accept, and agree that neither of them shall, at any time hereafter, seek or claim any spousal support or

maintenance of any type whatsoever, from the other party, because (1)
Nat has her own income, obligations to her children, and her own assets,
disclosed herein; (2) Les has an income and the savings disclosed herein;
(3) the parties have discussed the topic and depend on this clause as a
term and condition of their continued relations; and (4) the parties both
agree that it is fair that they provide this mutual release.

Again, this clause is inelegant, but it will very likely withstand judicial review.

Keep in mind, as well, that if your relationship endures for many years, the certainty that there will never be any support obligation may wane. For instance, parties who negotiated a prenuptial agreement in their 20s (providing for no spousal support) would probably expect enforcement if they separate at 31. If they remain together for the next 50 years, however, and then part company (say, because one of them suffers from dementia), the "no spousal" clause might be quite unenforceable, assuming that there are real means on one side, and need on the other.

Generally speaking, the courts try to encourage parties to freely enter into fair and sensible domestic contracts that are enforceable. The question of whether the court will show specific deference to a fair agreement is always dependent on the facts. A sensible agreement, that allocates risk, expense, and the reasonable expectations of the parties, is likely to survive review.

3. Property

Anything goes when it comes to describing how property will be owned during the relationship, how it will be handled, financed, and maintained, and what will happen if the relationship ends. Agreements which provide that "what's mine is mine and what's yours is yours — and anything we acquire together is ours" are typical, and commonly enforced because they are fair and reasonable. If that's the kind of "deal" that you want documented in your contract, you will likely find the Les and Nat example in the contract sample at the back of this book particularly helpful.

There are some exemptions to this principle, of course, but generally, the exceptions all arise because of fairness flaws. For instance, if the parties have agreed to keep their assets separate and apart, and they split up after four to five years, the agreement is likely unassailable. However, if they made that deal in 1965, and separated in 2005, at a time when one spouse had two homes and a million in cash (and the other spouse was disabled and penniless), the resulting variation is easy to imagine. Judges want to do what's fair and right, and they will, in a strong and persuasive case, upset an agreement to do "justice" and import fairness. Still, having a fair and sensible agreement that is clear and plain, and intended to stand the test of time, will likely lead to enforceability in the absence of egregious factual change.

4
Fairness

Your agreement must be fair. The fact that one party to an agreement says, in the throes of passion, "I'll never ask you for support" may be admirable (and even attractive), but it might not stand the test of time and it may not be enforceable in law. If your lover is disabled and needy, obtaining a written guarantee that things will never change probably will not satisfy the "fairness" test. The deal you make should be objectively fair from all perspectives.

Usually, having a dispassionate observer (e.g., friend, coworker, lawyer, or accountant) look over the agreement in advance of execution will reveal the fairness quality. If your agreement does not look and sound sensible at the outset, it probably won't stand up when it is needed, and that defeats the whole purpose of the document.

No one can tell you what's fair in your special and specific circumstances. The concept of fairness is one that can only be explored through frank and open discussion and a careful consideration of all the possible and likely scenarios that may play out over time. The red flags on fairness very often consist of the following:

1. An absolute and unchanging provision that no matter what happens, neither party will ever pay spousal support or maintenance no matter what. There are clauses of this type "out there" in the real world, but whether they are reliable or not is a real question. This kind of provision may be entirely appropriate for older "second timers" with modest incomes and similar assets, but it's almost never going to stand up for a young couple embarking on an enduring relationship built on codependency with the prospect of new careers and opportunities.

2. A provision that promises that no child support will be paid or claimed. A clause of this sort may be contrary to law, and is almost never fair, except in special circumstances. If, for example, both parties have part-time care of a child, and a governing financial arrangement with that child's biological parent, a provision that neither party *to this agreement* will claim against the other may be entirely fair and sensible. An agreement that proposes absolute insulation from a child borne out of *this* relationship, however, is not likely worth the paper on which it's written. An agreement between parties cannot prohibit the court from making a proper order for support for a needy child. Moreover, the parents cannot bargain away the child's right to maintenance. Accordingly, if a child's support is a contentious issue in your new relationship, consider your options carefully, and plan to see a lawyer for at least an initial consultation.

3. A provision that is otherwise unenforceable at law. The terms of the contract must be consistent with other legal obligations. For instance, if Les and Nat have taken a mortgage to buy a house together, a clause in their Cohabitation Agreement which purports to bind Les only (for the payments) will be unenforceable against the mortgage company. The lender is not bound by that agreement, in part, because it is not party to it.

Other problem clauses can be imagined. The basic test, again, is fairness. If your agreement is "out in left field," feasts on the inequality of one bargaining party, or is otherwise simply "lopsided,"it is likely vulnerable to later attack, and not worth drafting. Use common sense, logic, fairness, and then have it read by an objective third party. Perhaps you don't need a lawyer, just a sober friend with an open mind.

5
Other Grounds to Consider

Quite apart from fairness issues, there are, in the case law, other grounds for setting aside contracts, and having a marriage contract or another agreement declared void. We won't get too excited about these here, because they are peculiar, unusual, and uncommon, but it's best to mention some of the obvious ones, which include the following:

- Duress

- Mistake

- Unconscionability

- Undue influence

- Misrepresentation

- Fraud

Understanding these concepts requires little legal imagination. We all know what duress is, which is compulsion by threat. Mistake is a material misrepresentation or misunderstanding about a significant issue or fact. A mistake about "legal rights" may be less problematic than a mistake about a significant fact, but eventually, it all comes down to fairness. For your agreement to stand the test of time, it needs to be fair. If one or both of the contracting parties is mistaken about the terms of the deal, it's probably not going to stand up. That's true as well, where there is importuning (pressure), a misrepresentation about a material fact or circumstance, or a deliberate fraud perpetrated for an advantage. Where these elements are present in the negotiation process, or at the time of execution, they probably spell trouble. However, if your agreement is fair, and sensible, but contains a typographical error respecting pagination, and describes the Volkswagen as blue not green, it's not the end of the world. Common sense and fairness have a prominent role in law.

Having said all that, there are several areas where serious and important "mistakes" commonly occur.

Often, parties do not understand or correctly describe the circumstances of property ownership. This can be troublesome, so particular care is required. Sometimes, the confusion arises because parties just don't know the particulars, don't care, or do not appreciate the different ways to structure legal ownership. Often, a party who may believe he or she owns a vehicle or a property of some sort is surprised to learn that, in law, the property is owned by a corporation, or that it's leased.

Individuals and corporations can be registered owners of property in several different ways. How the property registration is recorded can be of enormous legal consequence. If ownership of a house, vehicle, recreational property, or any other significant asset is at stake in your case, make sure you find out about the particulars of ownership before you sign the agreement. If you are not sure, or just don't understand, talk to a lawyer and get your facts straight in advance.

The same goes for corporations and businesses. There is a huge distinction in law between a partnership, a corporation, and a sole proprietorship. If one of the parties to the agreement is involved in a business association involving any one of those entities, it will be critical to understand the legal position and circumstances before the deal is done. Having a lover "sign off" and release all claims against "Nat's business" may be enough to save a partnership or a proprietorship, but it might not reach as far as Nat's corporate shareholdings. In such matters, there's no substitution for clarity and certainty.

A further minefield exists with respect to pensions. Because an employer-sponsored pension has present value as a capital asset, but also includes an entitlement to a future stream of income, it is a legal "thing" of unusual legal and economic value. Beneficiaries are very often entitled to all sorts of pension benefits, and may, on retirement or disability, obtain health and welfare coverage, income, and (perhaps, for their surviving spouse) survivor benefits. If you are entering into a romantic relationship and wish to define the arrangement in a contract, it will be important to understand what pension benefits belong to you and your spouse. Keep in mind that the value of a pension is not simply the sum of the contributions made by the annuitant.

6

What Happens When One Partner Dies?

If your relationship endures, one of you will doubtless die before you separate. Sorry, that's not "happily ever after," but close enough!

Given the inevitability of death, you should remember that a contract is no substitute for a properly drawn will. Anyone who possesses enough assets to require a marriage contract is well advised to also have a will.

You may choose to deal with your assets differently in the contract than you would in a will. For example, you may be prepared to leave your partner all or some of your assets if your relationship is ongoing at the time of death, but you could have different ideas if you separate before death. What you do with your assets and obligations on death is determined by law if you have no will, and by your will if you have such an instrument. What you do with your assets if you and your spouse separate will be determined by your contract.

Your contract and your will (ideally) will work together, and complement each other. A will is a statement by the testator (the person who made the will) that sets out how the testator's assets are to be distributed on death. It will also appoint a person to be in charge of the management of the estate after the testator dies. As such, it can be rewritten any time the testator has a change of heart. The will only reflects the testator's intentions. By contrast, a contract documents an agreement between two adult persons and cannot be unilaterally changed.

The contract is also a document which may bind the parties after death. For instance, your estate could be bound to continue to pay support to your spouse after death if the contract expressly says so. The obligation to pay support (from your estate, after your death) can be binding on your estate and your heirs.

Another example would be that you could include, in a contract, a term that would permit your partner to live in the family residence after your death. If properly drafted, that bargain would prevail (as a life estate) even if you had willed the title of the property to someone else. Your heir might well take title to the property, but that title would be subject to a life estate created by the contract.

The contract might also help you to preserve an inheritance for children of a prior relationship, by providing that all or some of your assets will be exempt from sharing in the event of separation or death. This, of course, is a major motivation for making a contract in the first place: Many parties want to "contract out" of prevailing laws and do not agree with the "cookie cutter" approach to asset distribution that is established by government made law.

You should also bear in mind that you can try to make arrangements in either your will or a prenuptial contract to provide for your survivors or your new partner. One option is to maintain appropriate life insurance to benefit your partner or your children. Care must be taken to insure that the disposition described in the contract or the will is consistent with the "beneficiary designation" recorded on the policy. It's wise to think carefully about this when drafting a contract or a will.

Remember that even if you both agree in your contract to exclude or limit gifts to each other in your wills, the court (in some jurisdictions) may still vary your will to benefit your surviving spouse. In these jurisdictions, the court possesses a residual capacity to "rewrite" a will that's unfair. Your contract, in those jurisdictions, may be a factor which the court will consider in determining whether or not to rewrite a will. It is therefore suggested that legal advice be obtained on this topic.

You should review your will from time to time, to insure that it's accurate, relevant, and fairly expresses your wishes. As time passes, the fairness of your estate plan will need reconsideration. For instance, it might be fair to leave your surviving spouse nothing if your death occurs 2 years into the relationship, but unfair if you and your spouse have been together for more than 20 years. As life's circumstances change, your will should adapt as well.

7
Drafting Tips

As we have stated previously, there is no specific "magic" to drafting a proper and enforceable agreement, but some general rules apply:

1. Put all the material terms in writing. Do not omit important issues simply because you think it's "understood."

2. Use plain language. Don't pretend to be an old Welsh lawyer!

3. Do disclose all significant assets and liabilities on the schedules. Do not include every pot and pan, but do include vehicles, pensions, credit cards, and stocks.

4. Describe the material terms once, and once only. Do not repeat. Do not repeat.

5. While it may be perfectly fine to use "ball park" estimates of amounts due on a credit card or a vehicle loan, don't guess on big assets. If it is important to describe the value of a home, get an appraisal or, at the very least, a realtor's estimate of value. It is not a science of perfection, but there needs to be a realistic estimate of worth.

6. Never agree to agree later. Clauses of this type are completely unenforceable. If you must include a dispute resolution mechanism, say that "the parties agree that in the event of a disagreement between them with respect to this agreement, they shall attend mediation before instituting any form of litigation."

When you think you have a good and final version of your agreement ready to be signed, take a deep breath, read it again (and read it a third time), and then make final arrangements. Consider whether it would be wise to have your important document reviewed by a lawyer. It's not necessary to do that, and the absence of legal advice does not automatically invalidate a contract. However, having a lawyer review your contract is a good move and can reduce the chance of later disappointment.

Once you are sure that you have done all that you can to insure accuracy and completeness, make arrangements to sign the document.

Keep these points in mind when securing witnesses to the contract:

• You will each need one witness. Never use the same witness.

• The witnesses must be sober adults and persons who can likely be found again (in the future) if need be. The local barista and your 90-year-old uncle are not good candidates; your realtor and middle-aged neighbor are better bets.

• The witnesses must both be adults and of sound mind.

Make sure that after the agreement is signed, you each keep an original version, and at least one other version is safeguarded (in a safety deposit box, or other secure location).

At this point, you can go off and enjoy your relationship. Good luck!

Sample Contract

CONTRACT

THIS CONTRACT is made in triplicate and dated the _5th_ day of ___May___, 20 _--_ . *(date)*

BETWEEN:

_____**LES ERIN SMITH**_____*(insert full name)* **of**

  _1234 Main Street_____

  _Any town, Any place_____

(insert complete address)

(hereinafter referred to as " _Les_____ ")

AND:

_____**NAT TERRI JONES**_____*(insert full name)* **of**

  _1234 Main Street_____

  _Any town, Any place_____

(insert complete address)

(hereinafter referred to as " _Nat_____ ")

Introductory Recitals

> *Note: Introductory recitals are often set out at the beginning of a contract. They are meant to provide background information and to explain in very general terms the topics that the parties are intending to cover and the reasons why they are entering into the contract. The introductory recitals are often set out in lettered, as opposed to numbered, paragraphs.*

A.   _Les and Nat_____ *(insert names)* intend to begin living together in a

committed relationship on _May 20, 20--_____ *(date)*.

OR

A.   _Les and Nat_____*(insert names)* have lived together since

_____ *(date)*.

2

OR

A. <u>Les and Nat</u>_____ *(insert names)* will be married

on _____ *(date)* and intend to begin living together at that time.

B. _____ *(insert name)* has the

following children from a prior relationship:

<u>Bobby</u>_____ *(name)* born <u>April 2, 20--</u>_____ *(date)*

<u>Anne</u>_____ *(name)* born <u>October 16, 20--</u>____ *(date)*

AND/OR

B. <u>Nat</u>_____ *(insert name)* has the

following children from a prior relationship:

_____ *(name)* born _____ *(date)*

_____ *(name)* born _____ *(date)*

OR

B. Neither party has children.

Note: The following would be included if you are planning to, or possibility might get, married at a future date.

C. It is intended that this Contract will continue in full force and effect should the parties

marry at a future date.

D. <u>Les</u>_____ *(insert name)* is a(n) <u>carpenter</u>_____ *(occupation)*

and has a gross annual income of $<u>60,000</u>____.

E.   __Nat_____ *(insert name)* is a(n) __nurse_____ *(occupation)* and has a gross annual income of $ __40,000___ .

F.   __Les_____ *(insert name)* has listed all of __his_____ *(choose his or her)* assets and liabilities in Schedule A to this Contract.

G.   __Nat_____ *(insert name)* has listed all of __her_____ *(choose his or her)* assets and liabilities in Schedule B to this Contract.

Note: It is essential to list all *of your assets and debts in the Schedules, not just those that you are intending to share or not share.*

H.   The parties are entering into this Contract to –

(a)   determine ownership, management, and division of all property either or both of them own at the time of this Contract or that they may acquire:

(i)   during the time they live together,

(ii)   after their relationship ends, and

(iii)   if one of them predeceases the other while they are still living together;

(b)   determine their responsibilities regarding children in the event of separation or in the event their relationship ends;

(c)   determine their support obligations in the event their relationship ends; and

(d)   avoid disputes and litigation in the event their relationship ends.

I.   It is the intention of the parties that this Contract shall be a complete, final, and effective settlement with respect to:

(a)   division of property,

(b)   maintenance and support, and

(c)   children.

J.   The parties wish to confirm that:

(a)   each of them relies on this Contract to be enforced according to its terms;

(b)   neither of them would have entered in to this Contract had it been anticipated that the other person would apply at any time to vary it.

K.   The parties acknowledge that each of them is prepared to abide by the terms of this Contract and each recognizes that –

(a)   the importance to each of them of being able to rely on the Contract far outweighs the risk that it may operate unfairly at some future date; and

(b)   the impossibility of returning the parties to the positions they occupied before they entered into this Contract would make any variation, however fair viewed solely in the changed circumstances, unfair on the whole because all dealings with their property during the course of their relationship will have been based on the binding nature of this Contract.

L.   The parties are aware the law provides for a judicial intervention in some circumstances if this Contract is found to be unfair now or in the future.

IN CONSIDERATION of the promises which the parties have made to one another in this Contract, the parties agree as follows:

TRUTH OF INTRODUCTORY RECITALS

1.   The parties each promise that the statements of fact contained in the Introductory Recitals above are true and acknowledge that the other of them is relying on them to be true in entering into this Contract.

WHEN CONTRACT IN FORCE

2.　This Contract shall take effect when both parties have signed it and it shall continue to be binding upon the parties during their relationship and in the event the parties shall separate.

HOUSEHOLD EXPENSES

3.　_Les and Nat_ *(insert names)* agree to maintain one joint bank account for the management of household expenses including such expenses as rent or mortgage payments; utilities such as hydro, phone, and cable; and expenses for food and household supplies.

4.　Based on their present circumstances, the parties agree that _Les_ will contribute $ _900_ per month into the account and _Nat_ will contribute $ _800_ into the account.

5.　The parties shall review and revise this arrangement as their circumstances change from time to time.

Note: The following should only be considered if you are living in a residence owned by one of you which is not to be shared in the event of separation.

6.　(**OPTIONAL**) In the event that _Les and Nat_ are living in a residence which is owned by one of them and not to be shared in the event that the parties shall separate, then the owner shall be responsible to pay the cost of any and all major repairs and renovations from time to time.

Note: Consider that equal contributions to household expenses might at first seem fair regardless of your relative incomes. However, in the event of there being a marked difference in earnings, it is suggested that this arrangement might operate unfairly over time as it might enable the higher earner to accumulate savings while the lower earner does not have this opportunity and, therefore, unequal contributions might be fairer in the long run depending on the circumstances.

Responsibility for household expenses should also be considered in the context of children from a previous relationship. For example, you might decide that a disproportionate sharing of household expenses is fair if one of you has children from a previous relationship and the other does not.

CHILDREN – PARENTING ARRANGEMENTS

Note: It is suggested that, even if you are planning to have children but do not yet have any, it may be premature to set out any terms in the contract for children who are yet to be born and where parental responsibilities have yet to be established, in which case the provisions concerning children in this contract can be deleted (remember to renumber the following paragraphs). However, in the event that one or both of you already have children at the time that you are making this contract, parental roles are likely to have been established and it may be evident with whom the children will be living with in the event of a separation, even though it is likely to be premature to agree to any specific parenting schedule.

7.   In the event that Les and Nat   shall separate, then Les's

     children shall live primarily with Les   and the parties will

     work out a parenting schedule that is in the best interests of the children at that time.

CHILDREN – CHILD SUPPORT

Note: Even if you have children together at the time you are making this Contract, there are likely going to be limitations on what you can reasonably expect to agree to for child support in the event of separation. Child support in Canada is based on legislation called the Child Support Guidelines *which, in general terms, provides a guideline of how much child support is to be paid, based on the income of the paying spouse and the number of children being supported. Consequently, if you agree that child support shall be payable in the event of a future separation, it would not make sense to try and agree as to how much child support would be payable but rather only to agree that it will be payable in monthly installments starting at the time of separation and with the amount to be paid to be determined at whatever rate the* Child Support Guidelines *require based on the paying spouse's income at the time of separation.*

8.   In the event the parties shall separate, _____ shall pay to

     _____ child support to be paid on the 1st   day of the first

     month after the parties separate and continuing on the 1st   day of each and

     every month thereafter for so long as the children shall qualify for child support. The

     amount of child support shall be determined in accordance with the Federal Child

      Support Guidelines   having regard to the paying party's income at the time of

     separation.

OR

Note: Where one of you has children from a prior relationship, you may agree that, in the event of separation, the nonbiological parent will never be called on to pay support for the biological parent's children. However, you should be aware that the courts retain authority to determine what arrangements are best for child support and may order the nonbiological parent to pay child support even if the biological parent has agreed in the contract never to claim child support. The fact that the biological parent agreed in the contract never to claim child support would simply be a factor for a court to consider in determining whether to order the nonbiological parent to pay.

8. In the event the parties shall separate, __Nat__ shall never be called on to pay child support for __Les's__ children. The parties acknowledge the authority of the court to determine what arrangements are in the best interests of __Les's__ children and understand that court orders may affect the arrangements of the parties for child support as stated in this Contract.

MAINTENANCE AND SUPPORT FOR EACH OTHER

Note: As there is a guideline for determining child support payments, there is also a guideline for spousal support called the Spousal Support Advisory Guidelines *(in Canada). This is a formula which was developed by the Federal Department of Justice to determine the amount and duration of spousal support payable between common-law or married spouses. The formula bases support on relative incomes of the spouses and other relevant factors such as presence or absence of dependent children and length of the relationship. Just as with child support, it may not be possible or desirable to try to determine how much spousal support would be payable in the event of a separation at a future date as this will depend on your circumstances at the time of separation which may be very different than your circumstances at the time of making the contract.*

9. In the event the parties shall separate and either one of them is unable to be self-sufficient, then the other will pay monthly support in an amount for a period of time to be determined by reference to the __Spousal Support Advisory Guidelines__.

OR

Note: Despite what we have set out above regarding the Spousal Support Advisory Guidelines, *if parties wish to try to quantify spousal support which will be payable in the event of a future separation, we suggest that you consider the following:*

9 (a). If the parties shall separate during the first __five (5) years__ *(period of time)* after they begin living together then:

   (a) neither party will claim support from the other whether lump sum or periodic, and
   (b) each party forever gives up any claims for support against the other.

9 (b). If the parties shall separate _five (5) years_ *(period of time)* or more after they begin living together, _Les_ shall pay to _Nat_ support in the amount of _1,000_ per month starting on the _1st_ day of the first month after the parties' separation and continuing for a period of _two (2) years_ *(period of time)* or until the date _Nat's_ gross monthly income equals or exceeds the monthly amount of support set out in this paragraph, whichever is the sooner.

OR

Note: The parties may agree, depending on their circumstances, that neither of them will ever claim support from each other in the event of a future separation.

9. _Les and Nat_ *(insert names)* agree that they each have the ability to support themselves financially without the help of the other and it is their intention that they will both keep working and being self-supporting during their relationship and in the event the relationship ends. If the parties' relationship ends, neither party will claim support from each other whether periodic or lump sum and each party forever gives up any claims for support against the other.

BANK ACCOUNTS

10. The parties may maintain separate bank accounts and joint bank accounts during their relationship.

11. Separate bank accounts will remain the owner's separate property in the event the parties shall separate.

12. Joint bank accounts will be true joint accounts so that the balance in any such account will at the death of one of the parties belong to the survivor or, in the event the parties shall separate, will be divided equally.

RESPONSIBILITY FOR PERSONAL DEBTS

13. Both while the parties are living together and in the event they shall separate,
     <u>Les</u> shall be solely responsible for paying any personal debts
     and liabilities that <u>Les</u> may owe from time to time,
     including but not limited to those described in Schedule A.

14. Both while the parties are living together and in the event of separation,
     <u>Nat</u> shall be solely responsible for paying any personal
     debts and liabilities that <u>Nat</u> may owe from time to time,
     including but not limited to those described in Schedule B.

15. Neither party will, without the written consent of the other party, use funds from the
     parties' joint accounts to pay personal debts.

16. In the event of separation, each party shall be financially responsible for
     <u>Fifty percent (50%)</u> of any jointly acquired or jointly held debts
     regardless of the initial or ongoing proportion of each party's borrowed amount, unless
     the parties otherwise agree in writing.

Note: In regards to jointly held debts, it should also be noted that, rather than agreeing to share responsibility 50/50, it might seem fairer that each of you would be responsible for only that portion which each of you actually borrowed. However, then you would have to keep track of who borrowed what, which may prove to be difficult and presumably a joyless activity.

PROPERTY

All Property to be Divided

Note: You may decide that in the event you separate, you will not keep any of your assets as separate and that they will all be divided equally, in which case we suggest you consider the following:

17.   In the event the parties shall separate, they shall divide all their assets equally between them regardless of which of them is the owner or when it was acquired.

OR

Separate Property

> *Note: You may also wish to distinguish between assets you are prepared to share and assets which continue to be your property in the event of separation. We have called these "Shared Property" and "Separate Property."*

17.   In the event the parties shall separate, each party shall retain that party's "Separate Property," as described in this Contract, free from any claims from the other party.

18.   "Separate Property" includes:

   (a)   all of the assets listed in Schedule A are the Separate Property of
   __Les__ and all of the assets listed in Schedule B are the
   Separate Property of _Nat_;

   (b)   any inheritance or award for a personal injury claim shall be the Separate Property of the party who receives it;

   (c)   any gifts which __Les and Nat__ may give to one another shall become the recipient's Separate Property;

   (d)   unless a third party specifically provides to the contrary, a gift from a third party is the recipient's Separate Property. If the third party makes a gift to both
   __Les and Nat__, then that gift shall be "Shared Property," as defined below, unless the gift is from a third party who is the parent or relative of either __Les or Nat__, in which case the gift shall be the Separate Property of the party whose family member made the gift;

   (e)   Separate Property shall also include:

      (i)   any income produced by the Separate Property,

      (ii)   any increase in the value of the Separate Property, and

(iii)   any Separate Property acquired in whole or in part in exchange for the Separate Property or with:

       i.   the proceeds from the sale of the Separate Property or its substitute

OR

       ii.   the income produced by the Separate Property.

Shared Property

Note: In addition to deciding whether assets are to be "Separate Property," you are going to have to decide what will constitute "Shared Property" which is to be divided between you in the event of separation. We suggest you consider the following:

19.   In the event the parties shall separate, all "Shared Property," as described in this Contract, shall be divided equally between the parties.

20.   Other than Separate Property as described above, any asset acquired by either party while they are living together, regardless of who acquired it or in whose name it is registered, shall be Shared Property.

OR

20.   In addition to Separate Property as described above, any asset acquired by either party while they are living together shall be the Separate Property of the party who acquired it, unless it is registered in both parties' names or it recorded in writing that it is co-owned in which case it shall be Shared Property.

Note: You should also consider dealing with the possibility that while you are living together Separate Property may be used to purchase Shared Property and you might consider dealing with this as follows:

21.   Any Separate Property which is invested, used to purchase, or otherwise contributed to Shared Property shall cease to be Separate Property and shall become Shared Property, unless it is otherwise agreed to in writing between the parties.

OR

Note: As an alternative to distinguishing Separate Property and Shared Property, you might consider using some version of the following, particularly if one party has considerably more assets than the other.

21 (a). In the event the parties shall separate, __Nat_____ shall receive from

__Les_____ the following in full satisfaction of any and all claims of

__Nat_____ for division of assets:

    (a)   after one (1) year from the date of this Contract, $_____;

    (b)   between one (1) and three (3) years from the date of this Contract, $_____;

    (c)   between three (3) and five (5) years from the date of this Contract, $_____;

    (d)   between five (5) and ten (10) years from the date of this Contract, $_____.

21 (b). Other than as set out in paragraph 21 (a) above, each party shall, in the event that they separate, retain all of their assets free from any claims from the other.

Family Residence

Note: You may wish to deal specifically with your family residence as there will be issues of continued occupancy, both in the event of separation and in the event of death. We suggest that you consider the following:

22.   In the event that the parties are living in a residence owned in the name of

__Les_____ at the time that either of the parties expresses a desire to live separate and apart from the other, then __Nat_____ shall vacate the residence immediately. In the event that the parties are living in a residence owned in the name of __Nat_____ at the time that either of the parties expresses a desire to live separate and apart from the other, then __Les_____ shall vacate the residence immediately.

Note: Even if you are living in a jointly owned residence and one or both of you decides to separate, it may be better to have chosen in advance who will stay and who will go. In that regard, we suggest you consider the following:

23. If the parties are living in a residence which is jointly owned at the time the parties separate, then __Les__ shall vacate within __thirty (30) days__ of the parties agreeing or either party expressing a desire to live separate and apart.

Note: You might consider having the following provision to cover the issue of occupancy in the event of death.

24. If the parties are living together when the first of them dies (the "Deceased Party"), and the survivor (the "Surviving Party") is not sole owner of the home (the "Residence") in which they are living, the Surviving Party shall be entitled to reside in the Residence rent free on the following terms:

    (a) for so long as the Surviving Party wishes;

    OR

    (a) for _____ *(period of time)*;

    (b) while the Surviving Party continues to reside in the Residence, the Surviving Party and the estate of the Deceased Party shall share equally the cost of major repairs required to preserve the Residence, such as roof and exterior repairs, exterior painting, and major plumbing or electrical repairs; and

    (c) while the Surviving Party continues to reside in the Residence, the Surviving Party shall pay all taxes, insurance, water and sewer expenses, and all costs of maintaining the Residence except for major repairs required to preserve it.

Note: In the event you are acquiring the residence together, particularly if you are making an unequal contribution to the purchase, you may wish to consider the following:

25. In the event the parties' residence at _____ *(insert complete address)* is sold, whether during the time the parties are living together or upon their separation, the sale proceeds shall be distributed as follows:

   (a) to pay any and all applicable real estate commission;

   (b) to pay out and discharge any mortgage financing;

   (c) to pay any conveyancing costs and the usual adjustments on sale;

   (d) to pay _Les_____ the sum of $_____ representing _Les's_____ original down payment and to pay _Nat_____ the sum of $_____ representing _Nat's_____ original down payment; and

   (e) to divide the balance of the sale proceeds, if any, equally between the parties.

DISPUTES

26. (1) If a dispute arises concerning this Contract, the parties will use best efforts to resolve the dispute through mediation before taking court proceedings.

   (2) The parties will each pay half of the cost of mediation.

   (3) If the parties cannot resolve an issue that has been the subject of mediation, they will:

   (a) request the mediator to certify that mediation has failed on a particular issue before starting a court proceeding in connection with the unresolved issue; and

   (b) file the certificate with the court.

   (4) If either party refuses to mediate a dispute, the other party may take further proceedings to resolve the dispute, including court proceedings.

27. Unless the parties otherwise agree –

    (1) the law of the jurisdiction where the parties are residing at the time of separation applies to this Contract; and

    (2) the superior court where the parties are residing at the time of separation has exclusive jurisdiction over this Contract for all matters arising out of or connected with it, including the validity of the Contract itself, and no other action may be brought in any other forum, or subject to any other law.

28. If either party takes any court proceedings with respect to the property of the other or responsibilities to each other, this Contract:

    (a) may be filed or exhibited in the proceedings, and
    (b) will be raised as a defense to, and form the basis of a consent order in relation to any claim made in those proceedings.

GENERAL CLAUSES

29. This Contract benefits and binds the parties and their personal representatives.

30. For the purposes of interpretation, neither party drafted this Contract and its words are the words of both parties.

31. The headings in this Contract are aids for speedy reference, and have no legal significance. The headings are not part of the Contract and may not be considered for the purpose of interpreting it.

32. While negotiating this Contract, a variety of ideas and tentative arrangements were explored, but all of these are replaced by this Contract, which is the entire contract between the parties.

33.   The parties may vary this Contract only by a written agreement signed in the same manner as this Contract.

34.   Any reference to "when this Contract is signed" in this Contract means the date the last party signs it.

35.   If any provision of this Contract is invalid or unenforceable, the remainder of this Contract continues in effect.

36.   __Les and Nat_____ *(insert names)* will each do everything reasonably necessary to give full effect to this Contract.

WILLS

37.   While they live together and in the event that the parties separate, they shall each be at liberty to make wills leaving no portion of their estates to one another.

OR

37 (a). When the parties sign this Contract, each will also make a will naming the other as the sole beneficiary of that party's estate.

37 (b). In the event of separation, each party shall be at liberty to make a new will removing one another as beneficiaries.

OR

37 (a). __Les_____ will make a will leaving the following property to __Nat_____:

    (a)   __Honda Civic 2012_____ *(list)*
    (b)   __antique gold bracelet (family heirloom)_____

Self-Counsel Press/Contract for *The Prenuptial Guide*/SAMPLE CONTRACT — 2013-1

37 (b). ___Nat_____ will make a will leaving the following property to

___Les_____:

    (a)   ___silver men's watch (family heirloom)_____ *(list)*

    (b)   _____

37 (c). In the event of a separation, each party will be at liberty to make a new will removing one another as beneficiaries.

ACKNOWLEDGMENTS

38.   Each of the parties acknowledges that he or she:

    (a)   has been given the opportunity to obtain independent legal advice in respect of rights against and obligations to the other party under the law and this Contract;

    (b)   has read the entire Contract carefully;

    (c)   knows and understands the contents of this Contract;

    (d)   is signing this Contract voluntarily and without any improper influence exercised by anyone;

    (e)   has fully disclosed to the other all that party owns, all that party's debts, and what that party earns;

    (f)   is satisfied that this Contract provides adequately for personal present and future needs;

    (g)   after the terms of this Contract are carried out, will be able to pay current and reasonably foreseeable debts and obligations as they fall due;

    (h)   believes that this Contract will not result in circumstances that are unconscionable or unfair to the other party; and

    (i)   understands that the provisions of this Contract, if considered by a court to be substantially unfair due to the nondisclosure of a material fact, may be reviewed and varied by the Court despite the mutual agreement of the parties that this Contract is final and binding.

IN WITNESS WHEREOF the parties have hereunto set their hands as of the dates inscribed at a place within British Columbia _____ *(insert state, province, or territory).*

SIGNED, SEALED AND DELIVERED by   )
_____ in the presence of:)
)
)   _____
_____   )   *(signature)*
Witness *(signature)*   )
 Joe Smith _____   )   Les Erin Smith _____
(print name)   )   *(print name)*
 567 Main Street _____   )
(address)   )
 Any town, Any place _____   )
)
 Plumber _____   )
(occupation)   )

SIGNED, SEALED AND DELIVERED by   )
_____ in the presence of:)
)
)   _____
_____   )   *(signature)*
Witness *(signature)*   )
 Kim Jones _____   )   Nat Terri Jones _____
(print name)   )   *(print name)*
 888 Main Street _____   )
(address)   )
 Any town, Any place _____   )
)
 Real Estate Agent _____   )
(occupation)   )

SCHEDULE A

ASSETS AND DEBTS OF   <u>LES ERIN SMITH</u>

ASSETS:
(list)

1.   <u>Honda Civic 2012</u>

2.   <u>Antique gold bracelet (family heirloom)</u>

3.   <u>Sailboat</u>

4.   <u> </u>

5.   <u> </u>

DEBTS:
(list)

1.   <u>$15,000 vehicle loan</u>

2.   <u> </u>

3.   <u> </u>

4.   <u> </u>

5.   <u> </u>

SCHEDULE B

ASSETS AND DEBTS OF NAT TERRI JONES

ASSETS:
(list)

1.   Silver men's watch (family heirloom)

2.   2007 Honda Fit

3.   _____

4.   _____

5.   _____

DEBTS:
(list)

1. $2,000 Visa

2.   _____

3.   _____

4.   _____

5.   _____

Self-Counsel Press/Contract for *The Prenuptial Guide*/SAMPLE CONTRACT — 2013-1

Blank Forms

CONTRACT

THIS CONTRACT is made in triplicate and dated the _____ day of _____, 20___. *(date)*

BETWEEN:

_____*(insert full name)* **of**

_____

_____

(insert complete address)

(hereinafter referred to as "_____")

AND:

_____*(insert full name)* **of**

_____

_____

(insert complete address)

(hereinafter referred to as "_____")

Introductory Recitals

A. _____ *(insert names)* intend to begin living together in a committed relationship on _____*(date)*.

OR

A. _____*(insert names)* have lived together since _____ *(date)*.

OR

A. _____ *(insert names)* will be married

on _____ *(date)* and intend to begin living together at that time.

B. _____ *(insert name)* has the

following children from a prior relationship:

_____ *(name)* born _____ *(date)*
_____ *(name)* born _____ *(date)*

AND/OR

B. _____ *(insert name)* has the

following children from a prior relationship:

_____ *(name)* born _____ *(date)*
_____ *(name)* born _____ *(date)*

OR

B. Neither party has children.

C. It is intended that this Contract will continue in full force and effect should the parties

marry at a future date.

D. _____*(insert name)* is a(n) _____*(occupation)*

and has a gross annual income of $_____.

E. _____(insert name) is a(n) _____(occupation) and has a gross annual income of $_____.

F. _____ (insert name) has listed all of _____(choose his or her) assets and liabilities in Schedule A to this Contract.

G. _____ (insert name) has listed all of _____(choose his or her) assets and liabilities in Schedule B to this Contract.

H. The parties are entering into this Contract to –

    (a)   determine ownership, management, and division of all property either or both of them own at the time of this Contract or that they may acquire:

        (i)   during the time they live together,

        (ii)   after their relationship ends, and

        (iii)   if one of them predeceases the other while they are still living together;

    (b)   determine their responsibilities regarding children in the event of separation or in the event their relationship ends;

    (c)   determine their support obligations in the event their relationship ends; and

    (d)   avoid disputes and litigation in the event their relationship ends.

I. It is the intention of the parties that this Contract shall be a complete, final, and effective settlement with respect to:

    (a)   division of property,

    (b)   maintenance and support, and

    (c)   children.

J.   The parties wish to confirm that:

(a)   each of them relies on this Contract to be enforced according to its terms;

(b)   neither of them would have entered in to this Contract had it been anticipated that the other person would apply at any time to vary it.

K.   The parties acknowledge that each of them is prepared to abide by the terms of this Contract and each recognizes that –

(a)   the importance to each of them of being able to rely on the Contract far outweighs the risk that it may operate unfairly at some future date; and

(b)   the impossibility of returning the parties to the positions they occupied before they entered into this Contract would make any variation, however fair viewed solely in the changed circumstances, unfair on the whole because all dealings with their property during the course of their relationship will have been based on the binding nature of this Contract.

L.   The parties are aware the law provides for a judicial intervention in some circumstances if this Contract is found to be unfair now or in the future.

IN CONSIDERATION of the promises which the parties have made to one another in this Contract, the parties agree as follows:

TRUTH OF INTRODUCTORY RECITALS

1.   The parties each promise that the statements of fact contained in the Introductory Recitals above are true and acknowledge that the other of them is relying on them to be true in entering into this Contract.

WHEN CONTRACT IN FORCE

2.   This Contract shall take effect when both parties have signed it and it shall continue to be binding upon the parties during their relationship and in the event the parties shall separate.

HOUSEHOLD EXPENSES

3.   _____ *(insert names)* agree to maintain one joint bank account for the management of household expenses including such expenses as rent or mortgage payments; utilities such as hydro, phone, and cable; and expenses for food and household supplies.

4.   Based on their present circumstances, the parties agree that _____ will contribute $_____ per month into the account and _____ will contribute $ _____ into the account.

5.   The parties shall review and revise this arrangement as their circumstances change from time to time.

6.   (*OPTIONAL)* In the event that _____ are living in a residence which is owned by one of them and not to be shared in the event that the parties shall separate, then the owner shall be responsible to pay the cost of any and all major repairs and renovations from time to time.

CHILDREN – PARENTING ARRANGEMENTS

7.   In the event that _____ shall separate, then_____ children shall live primarily with _____ and the parties will work out a parenting schedule that is in the best interests of the children at that time.

CHILDREN – CHILD SUPPORT

8.   In the event the parties shall separate, _____ shall pay to _____ child support to be paid on the _____ day of the first month after the parties separate and continuing on the _____ day of each and every month thereafter for so long as the children shall qualify for child support. The amount of child support shall be determined in accordance with the _____ having regard to the paying party's income at the time of separation.

OR

8.   In the event the parties shall separate, _____ shall never be called on to pay child support for _____ children. The parties acknowledge the authority of the court to determine what arrangements are in the best interests of _____ children and understand that court orders may affect the arrangements of the parties for child support as stated in this Contract.

MAINTENANCE AND SUPPORT FOR EACH OTHER

9.   In the event the parties shall separate and either one of them is unable to be self-sufficient, then the other will pay monthly support in an amount for a period of time to be determined by reference to the _____.

OR

9 (a).   If the parties shall separate during the first _____ *(period of time)* after they begin living together then:

(a)   neither party will claim support from the other whether lump sum or periodic, and

(b)   each party forever gives up any claims for support against the other.

9 (b). If the parties shall separate _____ *(period of time)* or more after they begin living together, _____ shall pay to _____ support in the amount of _____ per month starting on the _____ day of the first month after the parties' separation and continuing for a period of_____ *(period of time)* or until the date _____ gross monthly income equals or exceeds the monthly amount of support set out in this paragraph, whichever is the sooner.

OR

9. _____ *(insert names)* agree that they each have the ability to support themselves financially without the help of the other and it is their intention that they will both keep working and being self-supporting during their relationship and in the event the relationship ends. If the parties' relationship ends, neither party will claim support from each other whether periodic or lump sum and each party forever gives up any claims for support against the other.

BANK ACCOUNTS

10. The parties may maintain separate bank accounts and joint bank accounts during their relationship.

11. Separate bank accounts will remain the owner's separate property in the event the parties shall separate.

12. Joint bank accounts will be true joint accounts so that the balance in any such account will at the death of one of the parties belong to the survivor or, in the event the parties shall separate, will be divided equally.

RESPONSIBILITY FOR PERSONAL DEBTS

13. Both while the parties are living together and in the event they shall separate,
_____ shall be solely responsible for paying any personal debts
and liabilities that _____ may owe from time to time,
including but not limited to those described in Schedule A.

14. Both while the parties are living together and in the event of separation,
_____ shall be solely responsible for paying any personal
debts and liabilities that _____ may owe from time to time,
including but not limited to those described in Schedule B.

15. Neither party will, without the written consent of the other party, use funds from the
parties' joint accounts to pay personal debts.

16. In the event of separation, each party shall be financially responsible for
_____ of any jointly acquired or jointly held debts
regardless of the initial or ongoing proportion of each party's borrowed amount, unless
the parties otherwise agree in writing.

PROPERTY

All Property to be Divided

17. In the event the parties shall separate, they shall divide all their assets equally between
them regardless of which of them is the owner or when it was acquired.

OR

Separate Property

17. In the event the parties shall separate, each party shall retain that party's "Separate
Property," as described in this Contract, free from any claims from the other party.

18. "Separate Property" includes:

(a) all of the assets listed in Schedule A are the Separate Property of
_____ and all of the assets listed in Schedule B are the
Separate Property of _____;

(b) any inheritance or award for a personal injury claim shall be the Separate Property of the party who receives it;

(c) any gifts which _____ may give to one another shall become the recipient's Separate Property;

(d) unless a third party specifically provides to the contrary, a gift from a third party is the recipient's Separate Property. If the third party makes a gift to both _____, then that gift shall be "Shared Property," as defined below, unless the gift is from a third party who is the parent or relative of either _____, in which case the gift shall be the Separate Property of the party whose family member made the gift;

(e) Separate Property shall also include:

(i) any income produced by the Separate Property,

(ii) any increase in the value of the Separate Property, and

(iii) any Separate Property acquired in whole or in part in exchange for the Separate Property or with:

i. the proceeds from the sale of the Separate Property or its substitute

OR

ii. the income produced by the Separate Property.

Shared Property

19. In the event the parties shall separate, all "Shared Property," as described in this Contract, shall be divided equally between the parties.

20.   Other than Separate Property as described above, any asset acquired by either party while they are living together, regardless of who acquired it or in whose name it is registered, shall be Shared Property.

OR

20.   In addition to Separate Property as described above, any asset acquired by either party while they are living together shall be the Separate Property of the party who acquired it, unless it is registered in both parties' names or it recorded in writing that it is co-owned in which case it shall be Shared Property.

21.   Any Separate Property which is invested, used to purchase, or otherwise contributed to Shared Property shall cease to be Separate Property and shall become Shared Property, unless it is otherwise agreed to in writing between the parties.

OR

21 (a). In the event the parties shall separate, _____ shall receive from _____ the following in full satisfaction of any and all claims of _____ for division of assets:

    (a)   after one (1) year from the date of this Contract, $_____;

    (b)   between one (1) and three (3) years from the date of this Contract, $_____;

    (c)   between three (3) and five (5) years from the date of this Contract, $_____;

    (d)   between five (5) and ten (10) years from the date of this Contract, $_____.

21 (b). Other than as set out in paragraph 21 (a) above, each party shall, in the event that they separate, retain all of their assets free from any claims from the other.

Family Residence

22. In the event that the parties are living in a residence owned in the name of _____ at the time that either of the parties expresses a desire to live separate and apart from the other, then _____shall vacate the residence immediately. In the event that the parties are living in a residence owned in the name of _____ at the time that either of the parties expresses a desire to live separate and apart from the other, then _____ shall vacate the residence immediately.

23. If the parties are living in a residence which is jointly owned at the time the parties separate, then _____ shall vacate within _____ of the parties agreeing or either party expressing a desire to live separate and apart.

24. If the parties are living together when the first of them dies (the "Deceased Party"), and the survivor (the "Surviving Party") is not sole owner of the home (the "Residence") in which they are living, the Surviving Party shall be entitled to reside in the Residence rent free on the following terms:

    (a)   for so long as the Surviving Party wishes;

         OR

    (a)   for _____ *(period of time)*;

    (b)   while the Surviving Party continues to reside in the Residence, the Surviving Party and the estate of the Deceased Party shall share equally the cost of major repairs required to preserve the Residence, such as roof and exterior repairs, exterior painting, and major plumbing or electrical repairs; and

(c)   while the Surviving Party continues to reside in the Residence, the Surviving Party shall pay all taxes, insurance, water and sewer expenses, and all costs of maintaining the Residence except for major repairs required to preserve it.

25.   In the event the parties' residence at _____ *(insert complete address)* is sold, whether during the time the parties are living together or upon their separation, the sale proceeds shall be distributed as follows:

(a)   to pay any and all applicable real estate commission;

(b)   to pay out and discharge any mortgage financing;

(c)   to pay any conveyancing costs and the usual adjustments on sale;

(d)   to pay _____ the sum of $_____ representing _____ original down payment and to pay _____ the sum of $_____ representing _____ original down payment; and

(e)   to divide the balance of the sale proceeds, if any, equally between the parties.

DISPUTES

26.   (1)   If a dispute arises concerning this Contract, the parties will use best efforts to resolve the dispute through mediation before taking court proceedings.

(2)   The parties will each pay half of the cost of mediation.

(3)   If the parties cannot resolve an issue that has been the subject of mediation, they will:

(a)   request the mediator to certify that mediation has failed on a particular issue before starting a court proceeding in connection with the unresolved issue; and

(b)   file the certificate with the court.

(4)   If either party refuses to mediate a dispute, the other party may take further proceedings to resolve the dispute, including court proceedings.

27.   Unless the parties otherwise agree –

(1)   the law of the jurisdiction where the parties are residing at the time of separation applies to this Contract; and

(2)   the superior court where the parties are residing at the time of separation has exclusive jurisdiction over this Contract for all matters arising out of or connected with it, including the validity of the Contract itself, and no other action may be brought in any other forum, or subject to any other law.

28.   If either party takes any court proceedings with respect to the property of the other or responsibilities to each other, this Contract:

(a)   may be filed or exhibited in the proceedings, and

(b)   will be raised as a defense to, and form the basis of a consent order in relation to any claim made in those proceedings.

GENERAL CLAUSES

29.   This Contract benefits and binds the parties and their personal representatives.

30.   For the purposes of interpretation, neither party drafted this Contract and its words are the words of both parties.

31.   The headings in this Contract are aids for speedy reference, and have no legal significance. The headings are not part of the Contract and may not be considered for the purpose of interpreting it.

32. While negotiating this Contract, a variety of ideas and tentative arrangements were explored, but all of these are replaced by this Contract, which is the entire contract between the parties.

33. The parties may vary this Contract only by a written agreement signed in the same manner as this Contract.

34. Any reference to "when this Contract is signed" in this Contract means the date the last party signs it.

35. If any provision of this Contract is invalid or unenforceable, the remainder of this Contract continues in effect.

36. _____ *(insert names)* will each do everything reasonably necessary to give full effect to this Contract.

WILLS

37. While they live together and in the event that the parties separate, they shall each be at liberty to make wills leaving no portion of their estates to one another.

OR

37 (a). When the parties sign this Contract, each will also make a will naming the other as the sole beneficiary of that party's estate.

37 (b). In the event of separation, each party shall be at liberty to make a new will removing one another as beneficiaries.

OR

37 (a). _____ will make a will leaving the following property to _____:

    (a)   _____ *(list)*

    (b)   _____

37 (b). _____ will make a will leaving the following property to _____:

    (a)   _____ *(list)*

    (b)   _____

37 (c). In the event of a separation, each party will be at liberty to make a new will removing one another as beneficiaries.

ACKNOWLEDGMENTS

38.   Each of the parties acknowledges that he or she:

    (a)   has been given the opportunity to obtain independent legal advice in respect of rights against and obligations to the other party under the law and this Contract;

    (b)   has read the entire Contract carefully;

    (c)   knows and understands the contents of this Contract;

    (d)   is signing this Contract voluntarily and without any improper influence exercised by anyone;

    (e)   has fully disclosed to the other all that party owns, all that party's debts, and what that party earns;

    (f)   is satisfied that this Contract provides adequately for personal present and future needs;

    (g)   after the terms of this Contract are carried out, will be able to pay current and reasonably foreseeable debts and obligations as they fall due;

(h)   believes that this Contract will not result in circumstances that are unconscionable or unfair to the other party; and

(i)   understands that the provisions of this Contract, if considered by a court to be substantially unfair due to the nondisclosure of a material fact, may be reviewed and varied by the Court despite the mutual agreement of the parties that this Contract is final and binding.

IN WITNESS WHEREOF the parties have hereunto set their hands as of the dates inscribed at a place within _____ *(insert state, province, or territory).*

SIGNED, SEALED AND DELIVERED by
_____ in the presence of:

_____
Witness *(signature)*

_____
(print name)

_____
(address)

_____

_____
(occupation)

)
)
)
)   _____
)   *(signature)*
)
)   _____
)   *(print name)*
)
)
)
)
)
)

SIGNED, SEALED AND DELIVERED by
_____in the presence of:

_____
Witness *(signature)*

_____
(print name)

_____
(address)

_____

_____
(occupation)

)
)
)
)   _____
)   *(signature)*
)
)   _____
)   *(print name)*
)
)
)
)
)

SCHEDULE A

ASSETS AND DEBTS OF _____

ASSETS:
(list)

1. _____

2. _____

3. _____

4. _____

5. _____

DEBTS:
(list)

1. _____

2. _____

3. _____

4. _____

5. _____

SCHEDULE B

ASSETS AND DEBTS OF _____

ASSETS:
(list)

1. _____

2. _____

3. _____

4. _____

5. _____

DEBTS:
(list)

1. _____

2. _____

3. _____

4. _____

5. _____